The
Connell Short Guide
to
George Orwell's

Animal Farm

by Zachary Seager

Contents

NOTES

Introduction

In 1943 George Orwell was working at the BBC, overseeing cultural broadcasts to India. He was living in a flat in Kilburn, West London, and contributing to left-wing magazines, newspapers and journals in his spare time. He had not published a novel since *Coming Up for Air* (1939).

Born Eric Arthur Blair in British India in 1903, he had been a schoolboy at Eton, a policeman in Burma, and a teacher in West London; he had written about the life of the poor in London and Paris, and fought in the Spanish Civil War (1936-9) as part of a Trotskyite militia. He had also written several novels – none them commercially successful – and published a great deal of non-fiction, mostly about social and political issues.

But in 1943 he wondered whether he would ever write fiction again. He was worried about money, and life in London was hard during the war. Then, finally, inspiration struck. He wrote to his friend and literary agent, Leonard Moore, in December, 1943: "You will be glad to hear that I *am* writing a book again at last."

Animal Farm was intended as an attack on Soviet communism and especially on Stalinism. Joseph Stalin (1878-1953) was a popular figure amongst the left-leaning British intelligentsia during the 1930s and 1940s, and Orwell hated this. It came as no surprise to him that when the novel was finished in April, 1944, nobody was willing to publish it. Anti-Soviet books were not in demand during the war, especially by Orwell's regular publisher, Gollanz, which specialised in radical left-wing literature.

When *Animal Farm* was finally published in the UK in August, 1945 and in the US in 1946, it caused a sensation: 4,500 copies were sold in the first six weeks, and nine translations were under way within the first eight months. More than a million copies were sold in the 1940s and 1950s, and by 1972 sales had reached 11 million.

The novel's commercial success was partly due to its propaganda value. In America, in particular, it became a weapon in the Cold War battle of ideas between democratic capitalism and totalitarian communism. The British government used it, too, funding a newspaper comic strip in the 1950s based on *Animal Farm*, which ran in, among other countries, Brazil, Burma, India, Mexico, and Thailand.

But *Animal Farm*'s success is largely attributable to its exceptional quality; it quickly became a classic of 20th century literature. No two books by a single author have sold more copies than *Animal Farm* and the Orwell novel which shortly followed it, *Nineteen Eighty-Four. Animal Farm* has been translated into more than 70 languages, and global sales are estimated at more than 20 million, making it one of the best-selling books in the history of publishing.

A summary of the plot

Animal Farm is set on the Manor Farm, a typical working farm in rural England run by Mr. Jones. Mr. Jones drinks too much, and neglects his duties towards the animals.

At the beginning of the book an elderly boar named old Major summons all of the animals on the farm together for a meeting. Telling them that humans are their enemies, he teaches them a revolutionary song called 'Beasts of England'. The animals are roused by old Major's speech, and they each go their way, singing their song and dreaming of a revolution.

Soon after the meeting old Major dies, and two young pigs named Napoleon and Snowball take it upon themselves to direct the other animals. They tell the animals to prepare for the great Rebellion, and together the animals revolt, driving Mr. Jones and his wife from the farm.

In celebration of their victory they rename the Manor Farm "Animal Farm", and establish 'Beasts of England' as their anthem. Immediately, they institute the "Seven Commandments of Animalism", which dictate that "All animals are equal" and that "Whatever goes on two legs is an enemy", but that "Whatever goes upon four legs, or has wings, is a friend". These Commandments are to "form an unalterable law by which all the animals on Animal Farm must live for ever after".

There is plenty of food and the farm runs

smoothly. Snowball, a very intelligent pig, teaches the other animals to read and write, while Napoleon, a "large, rather fierce-looking Berkshire boar... with a reputation for getting his own way", instructs a new litter of puppies on the principles of Animalism. Work is divided evenly, and everything is determined by committee. The animals are happy: they are free, and amongst equals.

The pigs, however, begin to separate themselves from the others. They set aside milk and apples for their own private use, arguing that the health of the pigs is important for the health of the farm itself.

Eventually Mr. Jones and his men try to take back the farm. Other local farmers support Mr. Jones, mostly because they are afraid of revolutionary activity on their own farms. The animals are prepared, however. Led by Snowball, who has been studying the battles of Julius Caesar, they at first begin to retreat. Mr. Jones's men sense an easy victory, and so chase the animals into the middle of the farm, at which point Snowball orders the animals to attack from all sides, forcing Mr. Jones and his men to retreat. The animals win the day, and Snowball is declared the hero of "The Battle of the Cowshed". The Battle is commemorated each year, alongside the anniversary of the revolution.

After the farm is secure, normal life resumes. Snowball announces his plans to build a windmill, acknowledging that the work will be hard, but arguing that in the end it will reduce the labour of the animals. All of the animals support Snowball's idea except Napoleon, who seems put out by it.

One day the animals hear a strange growling sound coming from the farmhouse. Suddenly a pack of dogs appears and attacks Snowball. They bite and scratch and terrorise the intelligent pig until he has no choice but to flee the farm. It quickly becomes clear that these dogs were the same puppies who Napoleon had instructed in the principles of Animalism.

With Snowball gone Napoleon begins to establish his supremacy. He replaces group meetings with a committee of pigs which will run the farm. He moves into Mr. Jones's old house and begins to adopt human habits such as the use of bed-sheets and the drinking of whisky. When the animals notice that Napoleon is breaking two of the Commandments of Animalism – "No animal shall sleep in a bed"; "No animal shall drink alcohol" – they go to refer to the Commandments themselves, which had been written on the side of a shed for all to see. The animals learn that the Commandments have been changed; or at least they think they have been changed, because they cannot quite remember the original wording of the Commandments. When the animals raise their concerns about Napoleon's behaviour, Squealer, a cunning young pig, claims that the Commandments have always been the same.

Napoleon announces that the animals are to build a windmill. The animals are struck by Napoleon's apparent change of heart, but Squealer says that the idea of the windmill had been

An artistic impression of the flag of Animalism - notably similar to the Communist symbol of the hammer and sickle. According to the novel, the green represents the fields of England, while the hoof and horn represents the Republic of the Animals

Napoleon's in the first place, and that Snowball had stolen it from him. The animals work hard, and progress is made on the windmill.

One night a storm comes and knocks it down. Napoleon says that the collapse of the windmill was Snowball's fault, and that he had been attempting to undermine Animal Farm. Moreover, Napoleon says, some animals on the farm remain loyal to Snowball, and these animals must be dealt with. Following Napoleon's orders, the disloyal animals are executed by the dogs. Soon it is claimed that Snowball had collaborated with Mr. Jones at The Battle of Cowshed, and that it was Napoleon himself who won the day.

'Beasts of England' is replaced with a song that celebrates Napoleon. Although not all of the animals are happy with what has become of the revolution, many of them are more concerned about Mr. Jones, worrying that the old farmer might take advantage of any internal division on the farm.

One day a farmer named Mr. Frederick attacks the farm in the hope of winning it for himself. Mr. Frederick's men are repelled, but the Battle of the Windmill, as it comes to be known, causes great damage to the farm. The newly rebuilt windmill is destroyed, and many of the animals, including Boxer, the hardworking horse, are injured.

Boxer had been instrumental in the revolution, and responsible for a great deal of the work on the windmill. But when, after the battle, Boxer collapses while working, Napoleon arranges for him to be taken to a vet. Benjamin, a donkey who "could read as well as any pig", notices that the van which arrives to pick up Boxer belongs not to a vet but to a knacker's yard. The animals are angry and confused. But Squealer says that the van had in fact been bought by the animal hospital, which had simply forgotten to repaint it.

A festival is held the day after Boxer's death, and the animals are told to follow his example and work even harder, for the benefit of Animal Farm.

Eventually the windmill is restored, and a new windmill is built. The farm begins to prosper, and the pigs increasingly take on the habits and mannerisms of the humans. Napoleon spends the money he earned from selling Boxer to the knacker's yard on whisky.

Many of the animals who had participated in the revolution die, and so too does Mr. Jones. The pigs begin to walk upright, to carry whips, and to wear clothes. The Seven Commandments of Animalism are reduced to a single phrase: "All animals are equal, but some animals are more equal than others." And Napoleon changes the name of Animal Farm back to Manor Farm.

At the end of the novel, Napoleon holds a dinner party in Mr. Jones's old house. The party is for the pigs and local farmers, and it is held in order to celebrate a new alliance between them. The other animals look in through the window and see the pigs and the humans drinking alcohol and playing cards together. They realise, finally, that they can no longer distinguish between the two.

What is *Animal Farm* about?

There is no mystery about this: *Animal Farm* is about the rise of communism in Russia and the political and social developments that took place in the early days of the Soviet Union.

Orwell acknowledged in a letter to his friend, the American writer and editor Dwight Macdonald, in December 1946 that his intention from the start was to write "a satire of the Russian Revolution". He even suggested that the French translation be titled *Union des républiques socialistes animals*, or *URSA*, an acronym which resembles that of the Union of Soviet Socialist Republics, otherwise known as the USSR. (*Ursa* is also Latin for bear, and, at least from the 16th century onwards, the bear has been a national symbol of Russia.)

Orwell's aim was to satirise the Soviet Union in "a story that could be easily understood by almost anyone and which could be easily translated into other languages". But why did he want to write such a story?

Why did Orwell write *Animal Farm*?

Orwell took great pains with his broadcasts at the BBC, always striving to make them popular; he was a little bored by the work, but not unhappy. Then, in 1943, the BBC handed out a pamphlet on wartime propaganda, which included advice for writers on how to deal with anti-Soviet feeling amongst the British populace. Orwell was enraged.

Although there was plenty of anti-Soviet feeling in Britain, little of it came from the left. As Orwell himself put it, amongst the left

Stalin is sacrosanct and certain aspects of his

policy must not be seriously discussed. This rule has been almost universally observed since 1941, but it had operated, to a greater extent than is sometimes realised, for ten years earlier than that. Throughout that time, criticism of the Soviet regime from the left could only obtain a hearing with difficulty.

Orwell found this attitude repugnant. He believed that Stalinism was reprehensible, and was appalled to see Stalin's supporters excusing the most egregious acts to uphold the good name of communism. As he wrote in his essay 'The Freedom of the Press', originally intended to be the preface for *Animal Farm*:

> At this moment what is demanded by the prevailing orthodoxy is an uncritical admiration of Soviet Russia. Everyone knows this, nearly everyone acts on it. Any serious criticism of the Soviet regime, any disclosure of facts which the Soviet government would prefer to keep hidden, is next door to unprintable.

Much as Orwell tried to persuade others on the left that Stalinism was wrong, his criticisms were deemed unwelcome.

When it came to Stalinism Orwell knew what he was talking about. He had fought in the Spanish Civil War in a militia loyal to the ideals of Leon Trotsky (1879-1940), and had written about the experience in *Homage to Catalonia* (1938). In Spain he witnessed the insidious way in which the Stalinist communists painted the Trotskyites as enemies and criminal subversives. He knew that they were being falsely accused, and that the accusations routinely led to the firing squad, so when he heard that Trotskyites in the Soviet Union were receiving similar treatment he had little reason to doubt such reports.

The British left had other ideas. And after 1941 so did the British government. At the beginning of World War Two, the Soviet Union signed a non-aggression pact with Nazi Germany, the Molotov-Ribbentrop Pact of 1939. In Britain, Stalin's apparent amity towards Adolf Hitler caused huge distrust, as did reports of state repression within the Soviet Union.

Then came the Nazi invasion of Russia in 1941. Suddenly Stalin had become Hitler's enemy, and Britain and the US found themselves on the same side as the Soviet Union. The three powers met in November, 1943 in Tehran, Iran, where they formally committed themselves to an alliance against Nazi Germany.

The British Government's Ministry of Information (MOI) – the department responsible for propaganda during World War II – continued to worry about public opinion, however, and with good reason. There remained a lingering distrust of the Soviet Union, and of Stalin in particular. The MOI produced a pamphlet for the BBC with instructions on how to remedy the public's distrust, which included, amongst other useful information, a guide on how to claim that the Red Terror was a Nazi fabrication.

The Red Terror was a campaign of mass killings and systematic oppression carried out by the Bolshevik communists: a minimum of 50,000 were murdered; many believe the true figure to be nearer 1.5 million.

Orwell was already sceptical about the Tehran Conference, noting, in his preface to the Ukrainian

ORWELL AND HOBBES

Orwell read widely and often turned to the 17th century philosopher Thomas Hobbes, whose views are like an undercurrent in *Animal Farm*. As Valerie Meyers notes, Hobbes's view of the world was diametrically opposed to Marx's. According to Hobbes in *Leviathan* (1651), the life of man is "solitary, poor, nasty, brutish and short", and all human beings are inclined to "a perpetual and restless desire after power, which ceaseth only in death".

For Hobbes, the one requirement of any government, of whatever kind, was that it be strong enough to hold warring factions in check. He considered it inevitable that society be divided into different classes. There are clear echoes of Hobbes in *Animal Farm*. In the last chapter, for example, Benjamin expresses the Hobbesian opinion that "hunger, hardship and disappointment…[are] the unalterable rule of life". Benjamin refuses to read, on the grounds that there is nothing worth reading. "The choice turns out to be a wise one," says Meyers, "when we consider how the written word has been manipulated by the pigs." ■

translation of *Animal Farm*, that he did not believe that good relations between the USSR and Britain could last. But when he saw the MOI's pamphlet, he was enraged.

Animal Farm was born out of his anger: towards the Soviet Union, towards the British government, and especially towards those on the left who supported Stalin. He would later maintain that the idea for the novel came from a simple event in his life. "I saw a little boy," he wrote in his preface to the Ukrainian translation,

> perhaps ten years old, driving a huge carthorse along a narrow path, whipping it whenever it tried to turn. It struck me that if only such animals became aware of their strength we should have no power over them, and that men exploit animals in much the same way as the rich exploit the proletariat.

According to one of Orwell's biographers, D. J. Taylor, Orwell had, since the start of World War II – possibly ever since his time in Spain – been "searching for a way to dramatise what he believed was the human betrayal practiced by the Soviet regime in the twenty years since the Revolution". Animals provided him with the answer. "We can readily grasp," says Valerie Meyers, "that animals are oppressed and feel it wrong to exploit them and betray their trust." And Orwell could count on us making common assumptions about particular species: "sheep and their bleating are a perfect metaphor for a gullible public... We commonly believe that pigs are greedy and savage..."

The novel took time to come together. According to Michael Meyer, a young friend of Orwell's whom he had met in the 1940s, the original scenario for *Animal Farm* was

a kind of parable, about people who were blind to the dangers of totalitarianism, set on a farm where the animals take over and make such a bad job of it that they call in the humans again.

Meyer recalled later that when the book came into his hands he was "staggered and delighted" that it bore no relation to this "awful summary".

In short, Orwell wrote *Animal Farm* because it was, in his own words, of the utmost importance "that people in western Europe should see the Soviet regime for what it really was". But behind this desire to expose the Soviet regime was Orwell's own commitment to socialism. He was dismayed by what was happening to the idea of socialism around the world, largely thanks to the atrocities and degradations committed by the Soviets. He wrote:

nothing has contributed so much to the corruption of the original idea of Socialism as the belief that Russia is a Socialist country and that every act of its ruler must be excused, if not imitated. And so for the past ten years I have been convinced that the destruction of the Soviet myth was essential if we wanted a revival of the Socialist movement.

Socialism has not enjoyed the rejuvenation he hoped for But *Animal Farm* has been extremely successful in its original aim: to destroy, in a story that could be easily understood by almost anyone, the pernicious Soviet myth.

Is *Animal Farm* an allegory?

In his essay 'Why I Write' (1946), Orwell describes *Animal Farm* as the first novel in which he had attempted "to fuse political purpose and artistic purpose into one whole". We have already seen his political aim; but his artistic aim was to present Soviet history in the form of an allegory.

Take, for instance, the promulgation of the Animalist ideology by old Major. Animalism is a stand-in for communism, and old Major bears a striking resemblance to the revolutionary socialist and philosopher Karl Marx (1818-1883). Similarly, Napoleon is meant to represent Stalin, while Snowball is a substitute for Trotsky.

Allegory in fiction is a story (or play or poem) in which the characters and events represent particular ideas or qualities. The concepts are usually related to morals, religion, or politics;

allegorical characters are not typically real people – or, as in the case of *Animal Farm*, not people at all.

One of the most famous examples of the form is Plato's allegory of the cave. In Plato's allegory, the philosopher Socrates describes a group of people who have lived their whole lives in a cave, chained up and facing a blank wall. There is a fire burning behind them; and the people watch the shadows projected on the wall by the figures that dance past the fire. The prisoners come to see the shadows on the wall as the true reality, and cannot understand that they are actually the imprint of another, greater world. The philosopher, on the other hand, can see that there is a world beyond the shadows on the wall. Thus, in his allegory Plato uses a simple narrative to convey a truth about the way we perceive the world.

Allegory, as this illustrates, can be used as a method of instruction. But it can also be used to convey ideas that, if communicated openly, would otherwise be censored or even violently opposed. In his book *Persecution and the Art of Writing* (1952), the German-American political philosopher Leo Strauss argued that writers often had to hide their most challenging ideas within their work. Sometimes things couldn't be expressed openly; they had to be expressed indirectly, or disguised, both to protect the writers and to ensure the survival of their work. This kind of indirectness, in the form of allegory, is precisely what Orwell used in *Animal Farm* to express ideas which he knew would be controversial in wartime London.

Why did Orwell have trouble publishing the novel?

Four publishers refused *Animal Farm* outright, including Orwell's regular publisher Gollanz and the London-based firm Faber and Faber. The poet T. S. Eliot, who worked at Faber and Faber between 1925 and 1965, wrote to Orwell about the rejection. Although he praised the writing and the book's "fundamental integrity" he objected to its overall message, which he took to be "generally Trotskyite".

He objected, too, that in the book the pigs were depicted as the most intelligent animals and therefore the most capable of managing the farm. It could be argued, Eliot claimed, that what was needed "was not more communism but more public-spirited pigs". (It seems that Eliot either did not perceive or chose to ignore the abundant irony in this sentence in Chapter Three: "With their superior knowledge it was natural that they [the pigs] should assume the leadership.")

Another publisher, Jonathan Cape, initially accepted Orwell's manuscript. But before publication Cape consulted with the MOI, and changed its mind. The novel was rejected. The publishers wrote to Orwell:

If the fable were addressed generally to dictators

and dictatorships at large then publication would be all right, but the fable does follow, as I see now, so completely the progress of the Russian Soviets and their two dictators that it can apply only to Russia, to the exclusion of the other dictatorships.

Research has revealed that the adviser with whom Jonathan Cape consulted at the Ministry of Information was probably a man named Peter Smollett, who was later unmasked as a Soviet spy. It was therefore not just in Soviet interests, but in Smollett's too, that Orwell's novel be suppressed.

Orwell himself, however, argued that there were subtler kinds of censorship at play. He wrote about his attempts to get the novel published in 'The Freedom of the Press': although the novel was refused by four publishers, he said, "only one of these had any ideological motive".

Two had been publishing anti-Russian books for years, and the other had no noticeable political colour. One publisher actually started by accepting the book, but after making the preliminary arrangements he decided to consult the Ministry of Information, who appear to have warned him, or at any rate strongly advised him, against publishing it. But the chief danger to freedom of thought and speech at this moment is not the direct interference of the MOI or any official body. If publishers and editors exert themselves to keep certain topics out of print, it is not because they are frightened of prosecution but because they are frightened of public opinion. In this country intellectual cowardice is the worst enemy a writer or journalist has to face, and that fact does not seem to me to have had the discussion it deserves.

The problem, in Orwell's view, was not the MOI itself. (He was no fan of that institution, however: it served as the basis for the Ministry of Truth in *Nineteen Eighty-Four*.) Although the shift in alliances that followed the Tehran Conference did not help matters, Orwell believed that the real issue was one of self-censorship. As we have seen, many of Britain's intellectuals were strong supporters of the Soviet Union, in large part due to the popularity of communism amongst the left. This led Orwell to write in 'The Freedom of the Press' that "the sinister fact about literary censorship in England is that it is largely voluntary".

Eventually, Secker and Warburg agreed to publish *Animal Farm*, and the first edition came out in 1945. Although space was provided for Orwell's preface, 'The Freedom of the Press', for some reason it was not supplied to the printer. This meant the pages of the novel had to be renumbered at the last minute.* The reasons for the mishap have

* The preface was not published until the 1970s, when the Orwell scholar Ian Angus found the original typescript in a desk drawer; he gave it to the author and political theorist Bernard Crick, who published it in *The Times Literary Supplement* in September, 1972.

never been clear, although it is interesting to note that in the proposed preface Orwell remarked that certain things were "kept right out of the British press, not because the Government intervenes but because of a general tacit agreement that 'it wouldn't do' to mention that particular fact."

If nothing else, the saga of *Animal Farm's* tortuous route to publication reveals, according to D. J. Taylor, "the practicalities of wartime publishing, the influences that could be brought to bear and the covert pressure that could be exerted without most observers appreciating that it even existed."

Why are Napoleon and Snowball enemies?

In a letter to Yvonne Davet, Orwell described *Animal Farm* as "*un conte satirique contre* Stalin" ["a satirical tale against Stalin"]. Indeed Napoleon is closely modelled on Stalin, despite being named after France's Napoleon Bonaparte (1769-1821). At every turn the rise of the pig mirrors that of the man, and there is a great deal of evidence to support this. One instance in particular shows how closely Orwell's view of the Soviet dictator informed his portrait of the dictator of Animal Farm.

Orwell had originally written that, during the Battle of the Windmill, "All the animals, including

Napoleon" took cover. Just prior to publication, however, he had this changed to read "All the animals except Napoleon". The dictatorial pig is transformed in an instant from coward to hero.

Orwell admitted that his emendation was made in recognition of Stalin's decision to remain in Moscow during the German invasion of the Soviet Union. The Nazis had made enormous strides into Soviet territory, and victory seemed almost assured. Stalin, however, stood firm. Soviet forces held Moscow and began a counter-offensive which eventually broke Nazi resistance.

Orwell's change of heart came after a conversation with Joseph Czapski, a Polish author and artist who was a fierce opponent of the Soviet regime. Czapski told Orwell that without "the character [and] greatness of Stalin" the Soviet Union would have fallen to the Nazis; Stalin had, in Czapski's assessment, saved Russia.

If Napoleon is an allegorical representation of Stalin, Snowball is a substitute for Leon Trotsky, and Snowball's rise and fall reflects the career of his real-life counterpart.

After initially working together to consolidate communist power in Russia, Stalin and Trotsky became enemies. Their antagonism stemmed from two sources. Firstly, it came from their respective ideologies. Trotsky believed in "permanent revolution", an idea that originated in Marxist theory and which, put simply, advocated communist revolution around the world, not just in one country.

After the failures of the communist revolutions in Europe between 1917-21, Stalin, on the other hand, argued that it was necessary to pursue socialism in *one* country, rather than to fight for revolution around the world. Once Russia was powerful enough, according to Stalin, it could then pursue communism beyond its borders. According to the Polish writer and activist Isaac Deutscher, these two rival ideologies were so powerful as to be "quasi-Messianic". This is mirrored in Animal Farm; while Napoleon argues that the animals must arm themselves to protect their new leadership, Snowball wants to send pigeons to neighbouring farms spreading the news about the revolution.

The second reason that Trotsky and Stalin became enemies was the power vacuum that followed the death of Vladimir Lenin, the first leader of the Bolsheviks, in 1924. They were the two most likely successors to the leadership, and both did their best to manoeuvre themselves into power. Stalin, like Napoleon, was the victor, and used his power to have Trotsky exiled and, finally, assassinated.

Orwell takes great care in *Animal Farm* to represent the subtle means by which Napoleon seizes power, and to show how Snowball's legacy, through the use of propaganda, is gradually altered and even finally erased. (Squealer says in Chapter Five: "'And as to the Battle of the Cowshed, I believe the time will come when we shall find that Snowball's part in it was much exaggerated.'")

Orwell was familiar with these methods from his time in Spain. On his return to England he noted that there were

> numerous sensible and well-informed observers believing the most fantastic accounts of conspiracy, treachery and sabotage which the press reported from the Moscow trials. And so I understood, more clearly than ever, the negative influence of the Soviet myth upon the western Socialist movement.

The experience taught Orwell a valuable lesson: "It taught me how easily totalitarian propaganda can control the opinion of enlightened people in democratic countries."

It is important to stress, however, that unlike Trotsky's followers, Orwell did not believe the revolution would have turned out differently had Trotsky, not Stalin, become the leader on Lenin's death. As Valerie Meyers observes, Snowball and Napolon are "equally bloodthirsty and immoral". When, in Chapter Four, Boxer grieves over the apparent death of a stableboy whom he has kicked in battle, Snowball urges him not to be sentimental, because "the only good human being is a dead one". Trotsky defended the killing of the Tsar's children, on the grounds that the murderers acted on behalf of the proletariat.

How close are the parallels between the characters in *Animal Farm* and real historical figures?

We have already seen the parallels between Napoleon and Stalin, Snowball and Trotsky, and old Major and Karl Marx. Other characters in *Animal Farm* also seem to correspond to real-life figures from Soviet history.

John Rodden argues that the cunning pig Squealer – who is said (in Chapter Two) to be able to "turn black into white" – can be considered a loose portrait of Vyacheslav Molotov (1890-1986), Stalin's head of communist propaganda. Rodden points in particular to Squealer's denial when other animals complain that the Commandments of Animalism have been revised. This was a common practice in the Soviet Union, and one favoured by Molotov. Indeed, after Trotsky had fallen out of political favour the evidence of his legacy was systematically erased.

But while Squealer can be seen as a portrait either of Molotov or of Soviet propagandists as a group, there is little doubt that the young pigs executed after complaining about Napoleon's takeover of the farm are based on Lev Kamenev (1883-1936), Nikolai Bukharin (1888-1938), Grigory Zinoviev (1883-1936), and Alexei Rykov (1881-1938). These once eminent communists were murdered during the so-called Great Purge of 1936-8, in which hundreds of thousands of people – possibly more than a million – were killed or detained as enemies of the state.

Some scholars have argued that each of the humans in *Animal Farm* corresponds to the leader of a European nation. It is very likely, for example, that Mr. Jones is based on Tsar Nicholas II (1868-1918), who abdicated following the February Revolution of 1917 and who was murdered, with his wife and five children, in July 1918. Mr. Frederick, on the other hand, is probably based on Hitler. Mr. Frederick invades Animal Farm, having previously sworn not to do so, just as Nazi Germany pledged to respect the borders of the Soviet Union prior to their invasion in 1941.

Other figures like Minimus the poetical pig – who writes the second and third national anthems for the Animal Farm after 'Beasts of England' is outlawed – are less clearly based on individuals, but are obviously borrowed from life in the Soviet Union. Many authors under Stalin became members of the Union of Soviet Writers, an organisation through which the Communist Party maintained control in the field of literature. Like Minimus, these writers were favoured so long as they held to the Party line.

Similarly, Mollie, the vain young white mare who leaves immediately after the Rebellion, can be compared to the old aristocracy in Russia, many of whom left the country after the fall of the Tsar. Likewise, the sheep can be seen as the apparently unthinking majority who – either too stupid, too lazy, or too cowed by those in power – support the status quo, however inhumane the actions of their rulers might be.

Other characters like Moses "the tame raven" (Chapter One) serve to illustrate Orwell's attitudes towards certain institutions. Moses is almost certainly the Russian Orthodox Church: it is no coincidence that Orwell chose a black-cloaked bird for his religious figure. Nor is it an accident that Moses has an obviously biblical name, or that he spends his time attempting to convince the animals that there is an afterlife in which they will no longer have to work. Moreover, Moses's flight from the farm mirrors the fate of the Orthodox Church in the early days of communist rule. The Church was abolished under the principles of the revolution; however, finding that worship had continued in secret, and that the support of the Orthodox hierarchy might be politically expedient, Stalin reinstated the Church, albeit with many of its privileges curtailed. In the same way Moses flies off after Mr Jones, only to return later, still preaching about Sugarcandy Mountain (or heaven).

Moses has also been compared to religion in general, about which Orwell was essentially scep- tical. Moses represents, according to Rodden, "the black raven of priestcraft – promising pie in the sky when you die, and faithfully serving whoever happens to be in power". As Orwell writes of Moses in Chapter Two, he "was Mr. Jones's especial pet, was a spy and a tale-bearer, but he was also a clever talker".

The critic Tracy Sutherland believes that Boxer, the loyal and hardworking carthorse, is based on the ideal of the Soviet worker represented by the Stakhanovite movement. Alexey Stakhanov (1906-1977) was a miner who achieved fame in the Soviet Union for his extraordinary feats of productivity. Alexey was held up as a model of the ideal worker in an attempt to increase the productivity of other workers. Thus with Boxer: after his death Squealer implores the other animals to recall the carthorse's motto: "I must work harder." The motto is designed to inspire both himself and other workers to even greater productivity.

Some critics, however, argue that Boxer represents the Russian working classes in general, who initially supported the revolution but were ultimately betrayed by Stalinism. In this reading, Boxer's going to the knacker's yard can be seen as mirroring the repression and callousness with which the Soviet proletariat were treated after the Revolution. Allegories are not always as straightforward as they might seem, and Orwell, after all, is writing fiction not history. But, as we will see, the novel *does* follow the history of the Soviet Union – and quite closely.

How do the events of *Animal Farm* relate to the history of the Soviet Union?

According to the novelist and critic Malcolm Bradbury,

> forming the backbone of [*Animal Farm*] was a sequence of direct if allegorised allusions to the betrayal of the Russian Revolution by Stalin and his acolytes: the treacherous treatment meted to Trotsky, the purges and show trials, the fudges of the Nazi-Soviet pact, and the exploitation of popular decency by a new élite for their own advantage and survival.

This is a comprehensive if abbreviated summary of the allegorical elements of the novel. But Orwell's attention to detail extended beyond broad brush strokes. The hoof and horn is a comic version of the hammer and sickle, the Communist party emblem; 'Beasts of England' is a parody of the 'Internationale', the party song; the Order of the Green Banner is the Order of Lenin. Indeed, the critic Jeffrey Meyers argues that "virtually every detail" of *Animal Farm* has "political significance" in relation to Russian history. Thus Mr. Jones's Manor Farm represents the political system of

FIVE FACTS ABOUT
ANIMAL FARM

1.

Since its publication, *Animal Farm* has been named one of the 100 best English-language novels by *Time* magazine, but some of its early reviews were far from glowing. *The New Republic* in America, for example, described it as "dull, inconsistent and full of stereotypes".

2.

Animal Farm first appeared in August of 1945, the same month that the United States dropped two atomic bombs on the Japanese cities of Hiroshima and Nagasaki, bringing an end to World War Two.

3.

Frances Stonor Saunders, in her "The Cultural Cold War", reports that after Orwell's death from tuberculosis in 1950 the CIA secretly bought the film rights to *Animal Farm* from his widow, Sonia. (who had become his second wife only three months before his death). The film, the first ever British animated feature, was released in 1954.

4.

Unsurprisingly, due to its themes, *Animal Farm* was banned by by the Eastern Bloc countries until the collapse of communism in 1989.

5.

Animal Farm has featured in a number of albums, including Pink Floyd's 1977 *Animals*, which was partly inspired by the novel. REM's "Disturbance at the Hen House" is also based on *Animal Farm*, and Radiohead's song, "Optimistic" contains a lyric mentioning the novel.

Poster for the 1954 animated film adaptation of Animal Farm

Imperial Russia, while Napoleon's Animal Farm corresponds to Stalin's Soviet Union. And "virtually every detail" extends as far as Orwell's methods of characterisation: Mr. Jones is irresponsible and neglectful of his animals, just as Tsar Nicholas was thought to have cared more for luxury than justice.

Chapter One corresponds broadly to the rise of Marxist ideology in Russia. The animals gather in the night to hear old Major's "strange dream", just as the early Marxists and communists shared their ideas in secret. And Mr. Jones breaks up the meeting with "a charge of Number 6 shot" just as the police attempted to suppress the spread of Marxism in Imperial Russia.

Chapter Two outlines the way in which old Major's ideas are elaborated "into a complete system of thought" by Napoleon, Squealer, and Snowball. This parallels the way that Marx's ideas were turned into doctrine by Lenin, Stalin, and Trotsky. And the Rebellion in Chapter Two – which

ORWELL'S EXPERIENCE

One reason we trust Orwell, says the American academic Peter Firchow, is our sense that what he writes is "authentic". There is good reason for this.

He had lived rough in London and worked as a dishwasher in Paris (experiences reflected in an early book); he had raised animals; he had experienced at first hand how brutally the Stalinist Communist Party operated in Spain.

In other words, George Orwell's books always rest on a solid foundation of lived experience. Though he is not is precipitated largely by the animals' frustration with Mr. Jones's neglect – mirrors the path to revolution in Imperial Russia during World War One, when food was scarce and the people were desperate for an end to their suffering.

The Rebellion is, in the end, "achieved much earlier than expected", just as the Bolshevik revolution took many people by surprise. And Napoleon's appropriation of the milk – "'Never mind the milk, comrades!' cried Napoleon, placing himself in front of the buckets. 'That will be attended to'" – parallels the pitiless suppression of the 1921 Kronstadt rebellion by the Bolsheviks, in which thousands of sailors and armed citizens were killed by the Red Army for rising up against the party. The same is true of Napoleon's appropriation of the apples in Chapter Three. Orwell admitted to his friend the editor Dwight Macdonald that he intended this to be the "turning-point of the story"; he even told the author and anthropologist Geoffrey

afraid to generalize or criticize others from the perspective of that experience, he is never a mere windbag or "theoretician". When he notoriously censured W.H. Auden for justifying "necessary murders" during the Spanish War though Auden had never witnessed an actual murder himself, Orwell could point out that he, on the other hand, had experienced murder and not just killing (in Spain and probably in Burma too). By doing so he was claiming the authority of experience over mere theory. "So much of left-wing thought," he went on to generalize about what he took at the time to be martini-Marxists like Auden, "was a kind of playing with fire by people who don't even know that fire is hot." ■

Gorer that this was the "key passage" in the novel.

Much of Chapter Three concerns the day-to-day affairs on the Farm, and mirrors the gradual erosion of revolutionary ideals that took place in the Soviet Union in the 1920s and 1930s. It was a fearful period in which the people were instructed to worry more about the dangers of invasion by a foreign power than to care for the daily degradations perpetrated by the regime. Squealer simply has to ask: "surely there is no one among you who wants to see Jones come back?" And to this the animals have "no more to say".

Mr. Jones's attempt to regain control of the farm in Chapter Four seems to correspond with the efforts of the Western powers between 1918-21 to defeat the Bolsheviks and restore the power of the Tsar, though there is some dispute about this. The critic and scholar Peter Davison believes that the Battle of the Cowshed represents the allied invasion of Soviet Russia in 1918. But the scholar and critic Peter Firchow argues that it represents the defeat of the White Russians – the party that opposed the Bolsheviks – in the Russian Civil War. In any case, Leon Trotsky's role was pivotal in both conflicts, hence Snowball's heroism at the Battle of the Cowshed.

Chapter Five shows the rise of Napoleon and his cronies, which reflects the rise of the Stalinist bureaucracy in the USSR. Napoleon's emergence as the sole leader reflects Stalin's rise to power, and the cult of personality that develops around

Napoleon parallels a similar cult that developed around Stalin. The critic Daniel Leab notes that the brutal repressions carried out by Napoleon's dogs parallel the practices of the Soviet secret police, and that the terrible treatment of the other animals at the hands of the pigs corresponds to the terror faced by the Soviet populace in the 1930s.

The gradual destruction of Snowball's legacy from Chapter Five onwards mirrors Trotsky's fall from favour; he goes from hero of the Battle of the Cowshed to "a dangerous character and a bad influence". Despite the fact that Trotsky had played a major role in consolidating Bolshevik power during and after the Russian Civil War, any evidence of his prominence was quickly destroyed after his exile, with photographs which showed him standing side by side with Stalin doctored so that he no longer appeared in them.

Daniel Leab also argues that the enormous efforts expended on the windmills are reminiscent of Stalin's Five Year Plans, in which Stalin attempted to industrialise and collectivise Russia with great haste. Millions of people died in the famines which resulted from these policies, and the deficit was made up by the use of prisoners who essentially worked as slaves. Thus in Chapter Six: "All that year the animals worked like slaves."

The critic Jeffrey Meyers argues that Napoleon's dealings with Mr. Whymper and the Willingdon markets in Chapter Six parallel the Treaty of Rapallo (1922), in which Germany and Russia renounced all territorial claims against the other following World War One. Meyers notes too that Napoleon's later dealings with Mr. Frederick mirror the Molotov-Ribbentrop Pact.

In Chapter Seven, when the animals confess their non-existent crimes and are executed, Orwell is alluding to the purges and show trials of the late 1930s, in which thousands of people were murdered. According to both Peter Firchow and Peter Davison, the Battle of the Windmill in Chapter Eight, meanwhile, represents the Great Patriotic War, which is the Russian term for World War Two. We have already traced the allegorical significance of Chapter Nine, in which Boxer is sent to the knacker's yard.

The ending of the novel in Chapter 10 reflects Orwell's view of the inevitable outcome of the Tehran Conference. Just like the pigs and the humans, the USSR and the West appeared to be on the path to reconciliation. Orwell, however, predicted that this allegiance would dissolve into conflict, and he was, of course, correct. As Jeffrey Meyers points out, Orwell's anticipated result is suggested by the deceitful strategies of both Napoleon and Mr. Pilkington, who "played an ace of spades simultaneously" in what was meant to be a friendly game of cards.

Virtually every detail of the novel has political significance, making it an extremely successful allegory of the Russian Revolution and its consequences. But is that all it is?

How does Orwell use satire in Animal Farm?

Since at least Aesop (c. 620-564 BCE) animals have featured as literary characters for both entertainment and moral instruction. Aesop's works are known as fables: short works of fiction which use anthropomorphism to illustrate a moral point, like 'The Tortoise and the Hare'.

Animal Farm undoubtedly has elements of fable. Indeed, the novel's full title is *Animal Farm: A Fairy Story*. (In the end this title was used only in Britain and in the Telugu translation which appeared in India.) The implication is clear: this is a book which, just like other fairy stories, has a clear moral message. However, just because Orwell called his novel a fairy story does not make it so. Equally, just because *Animal Farm* features talking animals that does not make it a fable. Beatrix Potter's *The Tale of Peter Rabbit* (1902), for example – which Orwell is known to have read as a child – famously features anthropomorphised animals; and yet it is not a fable.

Orwell's novel is not a fable either. Fables typically end with a simple moral lesson, especially one that can be reduced to an aphorism or maxim. *Animal Farm* provides no such conclusion: it is an allegory, not a fable; what it means is left to *us*, the readers, to decide.

Animal Farm is, however, a satire as well as an allegory, as Orwell intended it to be. Indeed

Malcolm Bradbury has called it "the most important work of fictional political satire to be written in twentieth-century Britain". Literary satire holds up to ridicule aspects of life: social mores, for example, or institutional abuses. It is chiefly comical, but it is often used as a form of social criticism, frequently with the intention of provoking change.

A famous example is Jonathan Swift's *A Modest Proposal* (1729) in which it is suggested that the poor sell their children to serve as food for the rich. Swift's satire censures the callousness of the rich, just as *Animal Farm* castigates the Soviet system.

Orwell admired Swift's *Gulliver's Travels* (1726) – it "has meant more to me than any other book ever written", he once said – and the fourth section of the novel serves as an important predecessor to *Animal Farm*. In Book Four of *Gulliver's Travels*, Swift reverses the roles of horses and humans, depicting horses as virtuous, rational beings and representing humans as depraved, irrational fools. Swift has been criticised for his apparent mis-anthropy, but his work has also been lauded as a satire on human nature in general.

By relegating humans to a supporting role in *Animal Farm,* and concentrating on the world of animals, Orwell, brought to his novel, argues Morris Dickstein, "a dose of Swiftian misanthropy, looking ahead to a time when the human race had finally been overthrown". In this view, the world of the novel becomes a kind of dystopia – an undesirable yet possible future which Orwell creates to highlight the dangers of contemporary life (just as he does later in *Nineteen Eighty-Four*). The distinguished American critic, Harold Bloom, also compares Orwell to Swift, especially in the opinion they shared of people in general. "Each loved individual persons," says Bloom, "while despising mankind in the mass."

It has been said of Orwell that he wrote sympathetically about human beings only when he presented them as animals, and there is some truth in this, thinks Bloom. Poor Boxer, the "martyred warhorse" is more lovable than Winston Smith, the hero of *Nineteen Eighty-Four*, while Mollie, "the flirtatious mare" is more charming than Julia, *Nineteen Eighty-Four*'s doomed heroine. "Even Benjamin, the ill-tempered old donkey, silent and cynical, and incapable of laughing, still becomes somewhat dear to us, largely because of his devotion to the heroic Boxer."

Whatever the merits of Bloom's argument about individual animals, however, the idea that Orwell found animals *en masse* more congenial than people falters when one considers that in the end many of those in his novel behave just like the humans – quite literally, in the case of the pigs – making it hard to make any real distinction between the two species.

Yet there is certainly a Swiftian edge to the satire in *Animal Farm*. The Canadian critic Northrop Frye sees it as adopting the classical formula of much literary satire, including Swift's: "the corruption of principle by expediency", or why the dream of a perfect world, a Utopia, will always end in tears. But unlike Swift, says Frye, Orwell doesn't seem interested in motivation: we never really know what the inscrutable Napoleon-Stalin actually wants. Orwell's point may be that like all tyrants all he really wants is absolute power, but *Animal Farm*, in Frye's view, doesn't make this clear.

Frye also took issue with the novel's ending, claiming that the moral of Animal Farm is "the reactionary bromide" that "you can't change human nature". But the criticism is not entirely fair, as Valerie Meyers writes: Orwell's purpose was to expose the totalitarian nature of the Russian government "in as simple and effective a form as possible, and in this he succeeded".

A measure of his success, perhaps, is evident in the way the novel was rejected by Jonathan Cape. *Animal Farm*, the publisher felt, follows "so completely the progress of the Russian Soviets and their two dictators that it can apply only to Russia, to the exclusion of the other dictatorships". However you label it – and it is part allegory, part satire, part fable and part dystopia – *Animal Farm* is an assault on the Soviet myth in particular, if not an attack on revolution in general.

What does Orwell think about revolution?

The animals were oppressed under Mr. Jones and they are oppressed under Napoleon. If anything, their lives are worse after the Rebellion. This, then, is an unforgiving view of the revolutionary process – and of the Russian Revolution in particular.

In 1944, not long after he had completed *Animal Farm*, Orwell wrote an essay about the Hungarian-British author and journalist Arthur Koestler. Koestler is today known primarily for his novel *Darkness at Noon* (1940), which tells the tale of an old Bolshevik named Rubashov who is condemned to death by a government which he had helped to form. It is, of course, an attack on Stalinism, but Orwell's essay considers Koestler's entire career up until 1944, as well as political literature more generally. Orwell writes:

> The Russian Revolution, the central event in Koestler's life, started out with high hopes. We forget these things now, but a quarter of a century ago it was confidently expected that the Russian Revolution would lead to Utopia. Obviously this has not happened... Perhaps, however, whether desirable or not, it [Utopia] isn't possible. Perhaps some degree of suffering is ineradicable from human life, perhaps the choice before man is always a choice of evils, perhaps even the aim of

Socialism is not to make the world perfect but to make it better. All revolutions are failures, but they are not all the same failure.

All revolutions are failures, then, even the ones that start out with high hopes. And yet, in his letter to Dwight Macdonald in December, 1946, Orwell argues that he meant the moral of *Animal Farm* to be

that revolutions only effect a radical improvement when the masses are alert and know how to chuck out their leaders as soon as the latter have done their job.

This mirrors one of the key themes of *Nineteen Eighty-Four*. In Chapter Seven of that novel, the protagonist Winston Smith considers the case of the proles – that is, the working classes, or, properly speaking, a group roughly equivalent to the Marxist idea of the proletariat.

If there is hope, wrote Winston, *it lies in the proles*. If there was hope, it *must* lie in the proles, because only there, in those swarming disregarded masses... could the force to destroy the Party ever be generated.

Orwell, like Winston Smith, maintained his faith in the working classes. This faith extended to his argument in 'The Freedom of the Press'. He wrote:

The ordinary people in the street – partly, perhaps, because they are not sufficiently interested in ideas to be intolerant about them – still vaguely hold that "I suppose everyone's got a right to their own opinion." It is only, or at any rate it is chiefly, the literary and scientific intelligentsia, the very people who ought to be the guardians of liberty, who are beginning to despise it, in theory as well as in practice.

The ordinary people in the street – the masses – the proles: to Orwell it was the ordinary people who held fast to the idea of liberty. As a "liberal moralist", in Harold Bloom's phrase, he was "grimly preoccupied with preserving a few old-fashioned virtues". His great concern was that the educated classes – the intelligentsia – would ultimately corrupt the masses, just as Napoleon and others corrupt the working animals on the farm.

In an article about her experiences reading Orwell, the novelist Margaret Atwood pointed out

ORWELL ON SOCIALISM

He hated communists, but, though a socialist, he could also be as vituperative about socialists as any Tory. He once described them, for example, as "all that dreary tribe of high-minded women and sandal-wearers and bearded fruit-juice drinkers who come flocking toward the smell of 'progress' like bluebottles to a dead cat". ∎

that in *Animal Farm* it is the average animal that suffers at the hands of the pigs:

> Though many characters are good-hearted and mean well, they can be frightened into closing their eyes to what's really going on. The pigs browbeat the others with ideology, then twist that ideology to suit their own purposes.

For Atwood, as for Orwell in *Animal Farm* and *Nineteen Eighty-Four* and 'The Freedom of the Press', it is the pigs' abuse and control of ideas and the power that they exert that finally subjugates the animals. As Atwood says: "it isn't the labels – Christianity, Socialism, Islam, Democracy, Two Legs Bad, Four Legs Good, the works – that are definitive, but the acts done in their name." In a sense, then, it does not matter that the pigs become like the humans at the end of the novel. The important thing is not the species but the method; and the pigs' totalitarian rule is merely a variation on an old theme.

Although *Animal Farm* was "primarily a satire on the Russian Revolution", Orwell confided to Dwight Macdonald that the novel was intended to have a wider application. That is how many critics have chosen to interpret the work – as an illustration of the pitfalls of the revolutionary process in general, rather than simply an indictment of Stalinist communism. Orwell was always fascinated by the corrupting effects of power, and of the relative weakness of ordinary people. But while

George Orwell broadcasting for the BBC in 1941

there was some ambivalence in his attitude to revolution, there was none at all in his attitude to the 1917 Bolshevik uprising. This, he said Orwell in his letter to Dwight Macdonald, was a "violent conspiratorial revolution, led by unconsciously power hungry people... *That kind* of revolution can only lead to a change of masters."

What is special about the style of *Animal Farm*?

Part of the reason for *Animal Farm*'s extaordinary popularity is Orwell's famously direct style; his preference, as Valerie Meyers puts it, for "grammatically simple sentences and unpretentious vocabulary". It is, after all, intended to be "a story that could be easily understood by almost anyone", as Orwell himself said.

In his essay 'Politics and the English Language,' published in *Horizon* in April, 1946, Orwell suggests that political language is "designed to make lies sound truthful and murder respectable, and to give an appearance of solidity to pure wind". He argued in favour of precision and clarity in language, claiming that vagueness was often exploited by those who sought to hide the truth rather than to reveal it:

> In our time, political speech and writing are largely the defence of the indefensible. Things like the continuance of British rule in India, the Russian purges and deportations, the dropping of the atom bombs on Japan, can indeed be defended, but only by arguments which are too brutal for most people to face, and which do not square with the professed aims of political parties. Thus political language has to consist largely of euphemism, question-begging and sheer cloudy vagueness... Such phraseology is needed if one wants to name things without calling up mental pictures of them.

Above all, Orwell argued that writing clearly is linked to thinking clearly; and thinking clearly "is a necessary first step toward political regeneration".

Orwell noted that he did not mean his essay as a critique of literary language. Rather, he intended it to be about "language as an instrument for expressing and not for concealing or preventing thought". Nevertheless, he set out six simple rules for good writing:

i.   Never use a metaphor, simile, or other figure of speech which you are used to seeing in print.
ii.   Never use a long word where a short one will do.
iii. If it is possible to cut a word out, always cut it out.
iv.   Never use the passive where you can use the active.
v.   Never use a foreign phrase, a scientific word, or a jargon word if you can think of an everyday English equivalent.
vi.   Break any of these rules sooner than say anything outright barbarous.

Although he was quick to point out that he himself was guilty of such infractions – "for certain you will find that I have again and again committed the very faults I am protesting against" – it is clear that Orwell had long held the beliefs outlined in 'Politics and the English Language'. Moreover, many of the themes in that essay anticipate the concerns of *Nineteen Eighty-Four*, and look back on the ways in which the pigs take control of *Animal Farm*. As Peter Davison has argued, one of the central points of Orwell's late political novels is "the capacity of language to erode independent thought".

Indeed, it is above all the linguistic failures of the animals that allows Napoleon to seize and abuse power. Squealer is able to convince the animals through a variety of rhetorical strategies that all is well on the farm, even when things are at their worst. It is notable, however, that Squealer's strategies are obvious to the reader but unseen by the animals. Take, for example, the Commandments of Animalism. It is the inability of the animals to commit language to memory that allows the pigs routinely to alter the Commandments, until the original message has been so corrupted as to be almost unrecognisable: "All animals are equal, but some animals are more equal than others." And if any animal raises a doubt about this manifestly unjust Commandment, the sheep are on hand to kill the conversation with deadening clichés and meaningless slogans.

Perspective and dramatic irony

The animals cannot recall what the Commandments of Animalism had once said: they only know that the Commandments do not seem quite right. The reader, however, knows exactly what has happened, and is incensed by the injustice.

This effect is largely achieved by Orwell's use of dramatic irony.

Dramatic irony is what happens when the significance of a character's speech or actions is known to the audience but unknown to the character concerned. The earliest examples of dramatic irony come from Greek tragedy, but it was deployed to astounding effect by Shakespeare. The audience of *Romeo and Juliet*, for example, know that Juliet has only taken a sleeping potion; Romeo, however, believes that she has committed suicide, and so chooses to kill himself alongside her.

The key to dramatic irony, then, is perspective. The audience knows that Juliet is sleeping because they were told beforehand about the sleeping potion. Here the dramatic irony is effected by the medium of drama itself; the audience sees a scene in which Juliet features but Romeo does not. In other words, perspective is not tied to a single character.

Many modern novels, however, tie their perspective to a single character, usually through first person narration or through a kind of third person narration in which the reader is privy to the thoughts of the character. When perspective is tied to a single character dramatic irony can be difficult to effect, because it is hard to provide the reader with information that the character does not already have. In *Animal Farm* Orwell uses an apparently omniscient narrator, allowing him to manipulate the characters to produce dramatic irony. There is an example of this is in Chapter Nine when Boxer is sent to the knacker's yard. The animals are too late to save Boxer, because they do not know what is written on the side of the van (until Benjamin comes along). The reader, however, knows precisely where Boxer is going.

What is interesting to note about the narrative voice of the novel is that it rarely enters into the mind of the pigs. Animals like Boxer are allowed interiority – that is, the reader is told what Boxer is thinking, and how he reacts to certain information – but the pigs are not (hence Northrop Frye's complaint that we never understand Napoleon's motivation). The pigs are divided from the other animals not only by their megalomania but by Orwell's literary technique.

What are we to make of Benjamin?

Benjamin is described (in Chapter One) as "the oldest animal on the farm and the worst tempered. He seldom talked, and when he did it was usually to make some cynical remark". His usual refrain (in Chapters Three and Six) is "Donkeys live a long time", which means that he is not particularly invested in the revolutionary novelties of the farm, recognising them for what they are: a moment in history that shall one day pass. The plot of Animal Farm has a circular movement: it ends where it began, with the animals, as Valerie Meyers puts it, "returned to conditions very like those in the beginning". To this extent, at least, the novel appears to endorse Benjamin's view that "life would go on as it had always gone on – that is badly" (Chapter Five). In fact it has been argued that very act of reducing human characters to animals, as Orwell does, implies a pessimistic view of man and of life, and that in Animal Farm the satiric comes very close to the tragic.

Benjamin is a sad figure, reminiscent of Eeyore in A. A. Milne's *Winnie-the-Pooh*. But the donkey's strength is his intelligence: he is the only animal wise enough to see through the lies of the pigs from the very beginning. Above all, Benjamin is described (in Chapter Three) as being able to "read as well as any pig". It is this linguistic savvy that eventually enables him to warn the other animals that Boxer is being taken to the knacker's yard; and it is this ability that leads him to shake his head each time the Commandments of Animalism are changed.

The critic Morris Dickstein has compared Benjamin to Orwell himself, and it is worth noting that Orwell's friends occasionally referred to him as 'Donkey George'. However, there is a crucial difference between Benjamin and George: namely, that Benjamin is content to despair at the state of the world, while Orwell was not. He might have had such an instinct; he often seemed depressed, and pessimistic. But despite this his career is marked by tireless political engagement and by an unending concern for the oppressed and the downtrodden.

Benjamin the cynical donkey ultimately represents a certain 'type', just as many of the other characters in *Animal Farm* can be taken as 'types'. Benjamin is the individual who views the world as ephemeral and therefore meaningless. Orwell, on the other hand, was of a different sort: he is often seen as a kind of visionary, a man who foresaw the 21st century and anticipated the dangers inherent in modern society.

Up to a point, at least, he was. But whatever we make of his predictions, there can be no doubt that he fought tirelessly for that fundamental human desire, the freedom from tyranny. And he was especially adamant to show, in *Animal Farm* and his other work of the 1940s, that our freedom rested to a large extent on intellectual liberty, and on the ability to speak freely and openly on all matters. As he himself put it in 'The Freedom of the Press': "If liberty means anything at all it means the right to tell people what they do not want to hear."

A SHORT CHRONOLOGY

1903 Eric Blair (later to become George Orwell) born in Bengal, India.

1907 Moves to England with his mother and sister.

1917-21 Goes to Eton on a scholarship.

1917 Russian revolution begins in March.

1922-27 Serves with the Indian Imperial Police in Burma.

1924 Lenin dies. Stalin takes over the leadership.

1927 Trotsky expelled from the Communist Party, to be exiled from the Soviet Union and, finally, assassinated in Mexico in 1940.

1933 Publishes *Down and Out in Paris and London* under the pen name George Orwell, while living in London.

1939 Stalin signs a non-aggression pact with Nazi Germany.

1940 *Inside the Whale and Other Essays.*

1941 Germany invades the Soviet Union in June.

1945 *Animal Farm.*

1949 *Nineteen Eighty-Four.*

1950 Orwell dies of tuberculosis while living in the Hebrides.

EIGHT QUOTES FROM *ANIMAL FARM*

All animals are equal, but some animals are more equal than others.

The creatures outside looked from pig to man, and from man to pig, and from pig to man again; but already it was impossible to say which was which.

Man is the only creature that consumes without producing. He does not give milk, he does not lay eggs, he is too weak to pull the plough, he cannot run fast enough to catch rabbits. Yet he is lord of all the animals. He sets them to work, he gives back to them the bare minimum that will prevent them from starving, and the rest he keeps for himself.

Four legs good, two legs bad.

The only good human being is a dead one.

No one believes more firmly than Comrade Napoleon that all animals are equal. He would be only too happy to let you make your decisions for yourselves. But sometimes you might make the wrong decisions, comrades, and then where should we be?

Several of them would have protested if they could have found the right arguments.

This work was strictly voluntary, but any animal who absented himself from it would have his rations reduced by half.

BIBLIOGRAPHY

Atwood, Margaret, 'Orwell and Me', *The Guardian*, 16 June 2003.

Bloom, Harold (ed.), *Animal Farm, Modern Critical Interpretations* (New York: Infobase Publishing, 2009).

Bowker, Gordon, *George Orwell* (London: Little, Brown, 2003).

Crick, Bernard, *George Orwell: A Life* (London: Penguin, 1980).

Davison, Peter, *George Orwell: A Literary Life* (London: Macmillan, 1996).

Davison, Peter, *The Lost Orwell* (London: Timewell, 2006).

Firchow, Peter, *Modern Utopian Fictions from H. G. Wells to Iris Murdoch* (Washington D.C.: Catholic University of America Press, 2008).

Leab, Daniel, *Orwell Subverted* (University Park, Pa.: Pennsylvania State University Press, 2007).

Lucas, Scott, *Orwell: Life and Times* (London: Haus, 2003).

Meyers, Jeffrey, *Orwell: Wintry Conscience of a Generation*, (New York: W. W. Norton & Co., 2000).

Meyers, Jeffrey, *Readers Guide to George Orwell*, (London.: Thames and Hudson, 1984).

Orwell, George, *Animal Farm* (London: Penguin, 2000).

Orwell, George, *A Life in Letters* (London: Penguin, 2011).

Orwell, George, *Nineteen Eighty-Four: The Annotated Edition* (London: Penguin, 2013).

Plato, *Republic*, trans. Desmond Lee and H. D. P. Lee (London: Penguin, 2007).

Rodden, John (ed.), *The Cambridge Companion to Orwell*, (Cambridge: Cambridge University Press, 2007).

Rodden, John, *Understanding Animal Farm* (London: Greenwood Press, 1999).

Saunders, Frances Stonor, *Who Paid the Piper? The CIA and the Cultural Cold War* (London: Granta, 1999).

Shelden, Michael, *Orwell: The Authorised Biography* (London: Heinemann, 1991).

Strauss, Leo, *Persecution and the Art of Writing* (Chicago: University of Chicago Press, 2010).

Sutherland, Tracy, "Speaking My Mind: Orwell Famed for Education", *The English Journal* 95 (1).

Taylor, D. J., *Orwell: The Life* (London: Chatto, 2003).